PRAISE 1

"Multiple reading _____ ...chel Mannheimer's thoroughly fresh debut reward and fascinate like multiple visits to Walter De Maria's eponymous *Earth Room* installation. This book is a charismatic travelogue for our interior and exterior landscapes; it's a conceptual art catalog with a poet's notes written in the margins; it's a one-act play of engrossing verbal theater. The stupendous *Earth Room* makes language a place. It's roomy, it's personal, it's every day."

— *Terrance Hayes*

"Rachel Mannheimer's *Earth Room* is something uncanny. Behold the odd charge in the atmosphere: one minute, your attention is carried forth by the poem's deftly calibrated details and riveting textures of thought; the next, you're inexplicably bereft, left with some dense, lush grief lodged inside of you. It's a feat the poem pulls off again and again: making traces of meaning felt, while leaving much unseen. Arrestingly peripatetic, *Earth Room* registers the body traversing and impressing upon the dense edges of psychic, physical, and imagined landscapes. And at each waystation and geographic marking, Mannheimer's warm, animating intelligence renews its insistent claim on life's blurriness and opacity. *Earth Room* is a wholly singular and lambent collection, made perfectly strange."

— *Jenny Xie*

"To describe Rachel Mannheimer's elegant, elegiac, and stunning *Earth Room*, I need to borrow the words an astronaut used to convey his first impression of the moon: 'magnificent desolation.' This is an intimate, understated, lunar-lit work of agonized earthen dispossession in which Mannheimer, in community, in grief, in love, and in solitude, acknowledges the very fine eroding line between art and life, and dares not only to cross it, but to do so with abandon. There is nowhere in this vertiginous work, as it takes us to memorials, galleries, performances, parks, guestrooms, seascapes, and cemeteries, in which the unbearable scale of human atrocity is not palpably encountered in 'direct, tactile intimacy,' and moreover, the magnificent desolation uttered in this haunted earth room is a wholly original confessional-ekphrastic undertaking that brings artifice and reality so close they speak with a single crystalline voice — Mannheimer's. This is an extraordinary book."

— *Robyn Schiff*

Earth Room

EARTH ROOM
A POEM

RACHEL MANNHEIMER

FOREWORD
BY
LOUISE GLÜCK

A CHANGES PAPERBACK

Published by Changes
www.changes.press

Design by Vance Wellenstein
Cover art: Score for "Trio B: Running,"
    from *The Mind Is a Muscle*, 1966–68, by the artist Yvonne Rainer
Printed in the United States of America

Changes Paperback #001

ISBN 978-1-955125-10-9

For my mother, Carol Moonie

CONTENTS

FOREWORD

This extraordinary book is as remarkable for what it refuses as for what it embodies. In a period that does not prize these virtues, Rachel Mannheimer writes with a clarifying cool detachment and calm authority. Make no mistake: this is a book of great ambition and unmistakable intensity of a kind we have nearly forgotten—to pay close attention is a form of intensity, a form that makes room for a multiplicity of tones, including sly wit. Mannheimer's subject is art. Not the art that endures unchanging in museums and libraries but the transient art of performance and installation, the mutable, perishable forms. We move in a kind of dreamlike suspension from one city to another, from the past to the present; works of art (Bausch, Rainer) develop and vanish. Mannheimer's immediate details are memorably sharp but the overall impression is of floating or drifting in the ongoing present of the poet and her partner. *Earth Room* is also a meditation on adult love, the companionship that originates in and protects solitude.

How many voices can sustain an entire book-length poem? I think of Claudia Rankine and Maggie Nelson. And here, Mannheimer, as she thinks aloud on the page with her supple, discerning intelligence. This is that rare work that is both profoundly alert to its historical moment and also, in the questions it entertains and the magnitude of its intent, timeless. It seems to me a lesson in how to make something of where we find ourselves.

Louise Glück

THE MOON

I'd never experienced virtual reality,
nor, I soon felt, had I ever experienced anything
so dazzling and hateful at once. The VR installation was called
To the Moon. It accommodated two
museum visitors at a time, and I'd made the appointment
so we could go together.
With my headset in place, the room was still there
but my body disappeared. The stool where Chris had sat beside me
was there, but Chris was gone. Then the room was gone
and I was alone on the moon. The feeling of transport was real
and the feeling of space—

But the attendant had promised flying—*just extend your arms*—
and it didn't feel like flying. It felt, crushingly, like I was missing out
on a major part of the moon experience.
There were ghostly dinosaurs on the moon,
there was a giant solitary rose made out of moon-rock and a donkey
that I rode along the surface of the moon.
I came to the edge of a crater and wanted to jump
but this was a passive section of the experience.

What did you see on the moon? I demanded as we left,
but Chris was experiencing nausea. He'd had a bad cold that week
so I'd been thinking about his death—
and now the aftershock
of my abandonment on the moon left me weeping.

What did you see on the moon? The attendant went in behind us
to wipe down the headsets, to welcome the next guests. I was angry
because this all felt like a vision of the future.
But maybe that's how people felt
when we landed on the moon.

Chris and I had both been granted residencies at the museum
for our writing, impossible luck,
and over the days had freely walked
through galleries that required no appointment.
But with Chris's illness, we'd been sleeping
in separate rooms, then going to our separate studios,
and now our separate moons—Chris flying and swooping
so dramatically you could vomit, while I stayed down on the ground.

That's how it was, sometimes, living with another poet.
Like we could both put on headsets and wave the controllers—
arms outstretched and triggers depressed—but for me alone
nothing happened. People say that poets love the moon,
but I got into poetry because I liked words and small things
and lacked the imagination for fiction.

There's a book my dad would read us
about a princess who falls ill
and won't be well until they bring the moon,
it's hopeless! But then someone asks
what she thinks the moon might be:
a disc of gold, no bigger than her thumbnail.
So, then, quite achievable.
But what will happen when, moon in hand, she sees the moon
still in the sky? It's fine—in her cosmology,
the moon grows back like a tooth. The book is called *Many Moons*.

Outside my studio window, dirty snow is piled up
around a pool of ice. When I arrived, it was liquid,
but it will be an ice rink soon—
I've seen them work, they hose it down to smooth it.
Now it's night. Two men climb into cars on either side,
their headlights meet across the ice. Now two visitors
approach on foot. Tenderly,
and not with their full weight—with one foot each—
they test the ice. The moon is far away
for all to see. I'm imagining the poems Chris will write.

The work would be about America. *We'll move around with open eyes, open ears, and our feelings*, Pina said.

The dancers had come from all over to join the company in Wuppertal, in Germany. Now in LA, they were dismayed: the lack of street life, everybody trapped in cars. Two vans would pick them up at their hotel and take them to rehearsal, pick them up. But they did go bowling. They sat in at a boxing gym and a UCLA basketball practice. They went to nightclubs and drag shows. They heard a gospel choir. They watched the gray whales heading south from Alaska.

In Pina Bausch's Tanztheater works, the dancers often make use of common props, break into song, and speak, addressing the audience. These theatrics might seem intended as populist, promoting legibility, but the actual effect can be unsettling. The bodies onstage are no longer attractive forms creating forms. They're people behaving strangely.

Movies! a woman cries. *I want to go to the movies!* A woman gets balloons stuffed down her shirt. A man wears a fox pelt as a loincloth and walks down a line of women in gowns; he's combing their hair. *As far as you can see, all this is mine!* A man drops a candy wrapper on the stage.

It's a common thing, how people feel invisible in cars. In high school, in Anchorage, driving my dad's Mercury, I often sang expressively and drummed the wheel. And when, home from college, I learned that Dan had slept with my best friend, I drove and parked and howled and beat the dashboard with real strength. It was what women do onscreen. It was instinctual. There, in the seat next to me, I'd taken his virginity the year before.

We did feel separate up there. America was my grandparents' houses, commercials during *Star Trek* for distant Olive Gardens, *New Yorker* reviews of museum shows I'd never see, and the J. Crew catalog—models in lightweight coats for winter, tailored and non-technical. I, too, visited Los Angeles and sat in back while others drove and didn't feel I knew it. I'd always accepted movies too easily as "real"— they overwhelmed me with emotion. I couldn't critically assess the artistic decisions made, had no interest in their making.

In Wuppertal, the stage was set with a stand of seven giant redwood trunks, shipped back through the Panama Canal.

Several paper houses get knocked down and rebuilt. A woman wears, strapped to her chest, two Big Gulp-sized plastic cups. A man wears, in similar fashion, a plastic clamshell takeout container, filled with live white mice.

Light cue. The redwoods look as though they're underwater. A fiberglass whale descends from the fly space. Hangs there like a train car.

Was it American? the *Times* critic asked two young German men after the show. They couldn't decide.

At the subsequent US premiere in Berkeley, some picketers outside protested the current state of funding for the arts. *Will Dance for Food*, one sign read. *Can't Afford to See Pina*.

P R O V I D E N C E

The day after we'd met—
in a bar where his ex-girlfriend was on stage—
I ran into him, asked for his number,
later texted
the only other Chris in my phone.

Hey, what are you up to?
He was sitting by a fireplace in Canada
with his wife and child.

I took a train to where
the new Chris lived,
in Providence, cried when he asked
about my mom, emphasized
my great love for my dad,
told him I had nothing going on
and didn't mind about the distance,
tore up several cocktail napkins
and left a pile of snow.

Then boarded the train on to Boston,
slept beside my childhood best friend
beneath a blanket
photo-printed with her face—
a joke-gift from her old love.
Dreamed that in my dreams I saw the future.

She had that pink Bruce Nauman poster
they used to give away at Dia: Beacon:
*Press as much of the front surface of
your body (palms in or out, left or right cheek)
against the wall as possible.*

Press very hard and concentrate.

...

I told her I doubted I'd see him again.

T E M P E L H O F

It's like the mountains, Chris said
about the open field. It was flat like a track—
had been a city airport—
and when you ran, you could always see
how far you had to go. There weren't many trees
and it was late for leaves, but there were birds.
The hooded crows were new to me—
hooded, I guess, for the black
that covered their heads, but it was the gray
down their bellies and their backs that was distinct.
They hopped around the baseball diamond, near first base.
Darkly, I had joked about the barbed wire curling
along the top of a nearby wall. But there actually was a camp here.
Forced labor for Lufthansa. Eleven were killed
in a Pittsburgh synagogue the morning we flew out—
the sanctuary where I might have prayed with Zev.
(I told him once I hated him. Stayed with him
for two more months.) All around Berlin,
there was considered signage about history.
I stopped under the banner for the home team—
Berlin Braves. Stern face
with familiar war-paint, feathers.
The boys on skateboards held surf-kites and sailed
down the former runway, toward the fenced-off section
where refugees were housed
in modular containers—a "container village"
is what I'd heard it called. Or they landed jumps
off granite slabs repurposed for the designated skatepark.
Beyond the fence, what looked like circus tents.
It was warm for November and women my age
draped overcoats over their strollers. Everywhere,
people whose judgment I trusted
were having kids. My oldest sister

had two little girls—sometimes slipped
and called them by my name.
I watched Chris up ahead—
now turning, now waiting, jogging in place.
I wished Mom could have met him. I held my arms out wide
in recognition. We were only in Berlin
these two gray months and wouldn't see
the light come back. We were having trouble
waking up, but we were trying to run
every day, to adjust.

THE CAR (MONTANA)

We'd driven through Butte, Wise River,
and Wisdom. There were signs for the Church
of the Big Hole. And then for the Big Hole
Battlefield, where we stopped. It seemed wrong
to call it a battlefield — the encampment on the field
had sheltered sleeping Nez Perce families
on a long retreat. After that, we just assumed
historic sites we passed were sites of slaughter.
I don't remember the name of the town
where we bought Diet Cokes, thumbed through
dusty bags of jerky. Chris asked the woman at the counter
how things were going. *Oh*, she said, *just crazy.*
We would see signs of fire, ashy trees on the mountain
like the ghost forests back home. We were in the basin
of the Big Hole River but I don't know
about the hole itself, whether it was behind us.

BEACON

She told me, Will said on the phone,
of the woman he had once described
as a "more feral" me, *that when she found out
who you were, she screamed.*

I knew how smug I was with Chris,
developing an interest in candles
for the home. It wasn't that I loved him more
than everyone before him.
But I felt now that people had been wrong
in emphasizing how much work
relationships required.

The days when he was gone,
I studied the squirrels
and my wall calendar
and felt as lonely as a mom.

Will and I had shared an office
and had a sort of joke
where we played at being office-workers —
mashing the keyboard like kittens, puppet-jawing
into the phone.

There was a skunk I also watched,
though I had thought that skunks preferred
the nighttime. There were no skunks
where I grew up and then, for a while,
I learned nothing new about animals.

BERLIN

The couch in our rental was too short,
so we built her a nest on the living-room floor.
She was a newish friend, and young, and we made a silly show
of being overly solicitous — keeping her
"always at the center of our thoughts."

We bought her dinner, took her ice-skating,
and in the morning rode the train to the botanical garden,
wandered the greenhouses. Fern house, cactus house,
bromeliads, Australia — the best day we'd had in Berlin.

She was spending the school year in Dortmund, a city known
for its Christmas tree. She said she'd watched them build it —
lashing lots of smaller trees to a giant frame.

Later, she stopped drinking
and cut off her hair. I worried I held
a version of herself
she'd never wanted shown.

WUPPERTAL

I'd watched the same program the year before
in Brooklyn with a friend.
He was a patron of the arts, in the monied sense,
and we had gone opening night—
along with several genuine billionaires,
pointed out to me
in the members' lounge at intermission.
Could I have identified them on my own?
By the shoes, maybe.

It's the Rust Belt of Germany, someone had told us.
Or maybe the Appalachia.

So, in Wuppertal, it was the same as anything:
familiar movements
with new people in the roles.
The set hadn't changed—
the dirt heaped on the stage,
sticking to the dancers' skin and sweat-soaked dresses.

They're not dancers. They're people who dance. Pina Bausch.
Brought to Wuppertal to direct
the local company, she'd overseen
a drop in subscriptions.

Bausch's works were developed
through what many would—though Bausch would not—
call improvisation, but,
once finalized, were fixed.
But the snapping of the strap of the smallest dancer's dress—
I don't think that was planned.
In the wings, she tied it back in place.

Transcript of symposium, comment from the audience:
What we see in Bausch is rage—the rage of a woman.
[Murmurs of disinterest and dissent]

Public transportation there
is by suspension railway. The cars hang in the sky
from a single rail.
An elephant named Tuffi once jumped
from a train car into the river below
and survived, delighting the locals.
Days after we rode, a section of the power rail
came crashing down.
The system was closed for months.

At the circus, after Christmas,
my niece was unperturbed
when we saw a woman balance in a handstand
on a plank
laid across the shoulders of two men riding bicycles
along a high tightrope.

T E M P E L H O F

A relationship is only that—
the space between two shapes. A shape.

Maybe Dan was right.
At the Gemäldegalerie, there were so many ways
to be a mom—so many babies one could have.
Botticelli's sweet, walleyed Maria,
the infant vain and knowing on her lap.
And then these Flemish babies—
one a jointed, bleached-wood doll,
one a hairless cat.

Madonna and child in the Maso di Banco
regard each other like a fond and fussy couple—
he reaches out as though to steal a morsel
from her plate. All their sons
died young and terribly.

Chris, in his orange hat, wandered back
from the landscapes to find me.

Why should I ever miss her less?
It's only ever longer since I've seen her.

PITTSBURGH

We hadn't spoken in a year
but Zev had met a girl I knew
from theater, as a kid. She'd called herself
"the only Jew from Alaska."

He had inside knowledge
that this wasn't true, and was an advocate
for facts —

Yes, she knew me — and my sisters!
She herself had two.
She'd made the statement whimsically,
said to say hello.

It was her birthday party where they met and so
one must make certain allowances. It's fine
to want to feel sui generis,
or to text an ex, who —
if we're getting into points of law —
may not count, actually,
being only really half
and on her father's side.

The grass is always greener in the cemetery,
was a joke I made to Zev. He said that was sick,
but he's the one who killed a succulent.

Browsing alone, I found a book of Robert Smithson's writings,
text designed by Sol LeWitt.
Smithson quotes Olmsted, regarding Central Park:
The museum is not a part of the park, but a deduction from it.
The subways, though, do not deduct —
they, like parks, allow escape.

Allan Kaprow called museums mausoleums.
Still, a park is art, not wilderness, where "man is a visitor
who does not remain."

For his *Glue Pour,* Smithson emptied a 45-gallon drum of glue
down a ravine in Vancouver. He pulled out the drum's plastic liner
and squeezed out the final drops.

ANCHORAGE

The story I took
from Sunday school was this:
God created the world, God parted the Red Sea,
and after the Holocaust, the British had some land no one was using
so they gave it to the Jews as a home.

The Territory of Alaska had been suggested as a possible refuge for German Jews as early as November 1938. A bill was introduced in 1940, pitched as an effort toward development: Refugee workers — allowed outside of standing federal immigration quotas — would further the project of resource extraction, processing gold and timber, manufacturing products from reindeer hides.

The bill died in subcommittee, having been staunchly opposed by Alaska delegate Anthony Dimond. What the territory needed for development, he argued, was roads, not refugees, and by letting in those otherwise barred entry to the States, Alaska would become a kind of concentration camp. Plus, Alaskans, on the whole, hadn't welcomed the proposal. They had concerns about assimilation.

A second measure, early '41, was similarly opposed. In letters collected by Dimond, Alaska residents expressed a wish for "white Americans of worthy stock." *It is hard enough to pioneer without having to combat hordes of aliens.*

At the time, white "pioneers" comprised only half the population.

Dimond would be honored with a major boulevard in Anchorage and a high school in his name. The shopping mall, I think, got its name from the road. It had an indoor ice rink and was where I saw my dentist as a kid.

My peers, the theater boys who sang the "Dreidel Song" at me—they didn't know enough Jews to form a stereotype.

Who, Hitler asked, *remembers the Red Indians?* He meant this inspirationally.

The other memorial at the entrance
to Weißensee Cemetery
is for 12,000 Berlin Jews who fought
in the First World War and died.
Inside, most of the stones are simple tablets.
Some rest on tree stumps also carved of stone,
like music on a music stand. Some have fallen off.
Some bourgeois families built impressive tombs.
A few large stones with family names have spaces
for family never buried here as planned.
On others, names were scratched in
with the death date and the camp —
someone returned. And there's a whole field
of urns. Early on, camp administrators
sent ashes back to families, for a price.
There were so many Jews before.
You feel their multitude in the cemetery's size —
so enormous that a few
who fled their homes and hid
on its vast grounds all through the war
managed to survive.

A second-floor loft filled with dirt up to the windowsills could look like disaster. Inside, the earth is damp and fragrant and feels newly claimed. Bill cares for the dirt— raking and watering, removing sprouts and fungi that might grow. *I used to only rake in one direction. Now, I also rake horizontally.*

Summers, with the *Earth Room* closed to visitors, Bill would "trench it up," find cracks in the sheetrock, let them dry to be repaired. Now the plan is to stay open all year round. I ask him how it's possible. *Who knows!* He has great eyebrows. A younger employee tells me: climate control, more tarps.

Technically, the *New York Earth Room* — third of Walter De Maria's "minimal, flat, horizontal earth sculptures." The first, at the Galerie Heiner Friedrich in Munich, opened in September 1968:

PURE DIRT ⁻ PURE EARTH ⁻ PURE LAND

NO OBJECT ON IT
NO OBJECT IN IT

It was installed for less than two weeks. *Or, if you ask Heiner, it's still there.*

A sign forbidding photography is being flagrantly ignored. Bill finally plucks up the sign and plants it in the dirt. I rarely feel a natural urge to take pictures, though I have been lately fighting a natural urge to obey.

In April 1968, De Maria sent a telegram to gallerist Virginia Dwan.

DEAR VIRGINIA MANY LAND SENSATIONS AND PROJECTS ALREADY REALIZED SO VERY POSITIVE I URGE YOU TO CONSIDER CLOSING OF GALLERY AND TO CONSIDER WORLD WIDE LAND OPERATIONS.

The second *Earth Room* was installed in Darmstadt, Germany, in 1974.

One can easily imagine it, Pina with her partner and collaborator, Rolf, who designed her sets and costumes, in Munich or in Darmstadt, looking out at all the dirt.

NO MARKINGS ON IT
NO MARKINGS IN IT

NOTHING GROWING ON IT
NOTHING GROWING IN IT

Bausch's *Rite of Spring* debuted in '75 in Wuppertal. Before the dance begins, dirt is dumped on stage from six big metal dumpsters, spread out by a dozen stagehands with brooms. The lights come up on a woman lying there alone.

I angled the trowel.
Dug up the shoots wherever
they had sprouted. Alien, invasive —
the metaphors weren't great.
They thrive by taking resources
from other plants.

The news from the border
was so plainly horrible
it was hard to understand.
A nation of immigrants! people always said —
a scrubbing of the slave trade, plus
I thought some liked the trick of it:
an immigrant who's white.
Besides, it's only after
rooting others out.

Non-native, like dandelions,
mice. There's still some debate
about horses. I didn't want to die
but I felt shitty in my living.
Every time we drove the car
or let the milk go bad, any time
I brought in from the mailbox
those envelopes with little plastic windows
for our home address.

I wanted to be
a steward of the land.
To eradicate the knotweed,
you had to tarp it over,
smother it. But it was spreading
from a grove across the fence.
I kept digging, I had told the landlord
I would do it. In exchange,
he knocked some money
off our rent.

B E A C O N

As I descended the stairs of the overpass,
glassed-in and greenhouse-hot, to access the platform
where I'd wait for the train, I saw the cars
parked in the lot behind me, reflected in the glass
through which I looked out at the river, so that
the cars were — all of them — submerged
below the water's surface, wavering.

Often, Chris woke screaming.
That night, he saw my ghost
in the corner of our room.

He called out my name
and since I was — in waking life —
alive, I answered him.

BEACON

Outside the house, I found I'd lost
even my ability to flirt. The more I tried to charm,
the more I felt myself adopting
Chris's intonations, his various little ways.
I repeated jokes. Everybody fell for him.

CAYUGA LAKE

We'd both moved east for college. At his school, they called him Alaska Dan. At mine, two hours north, I was largely unknown. I had, up till then, thought myself naturally outgoing, but it became apparent that had been environmental.

In college, we agreed that it was size. Any piece of art, made big enough, was cool. It was good to have a concept, but size could be a concept, or substitute for one. We loved Robert Smithson, art so big you could walk on it—a rock jetty spiraling 1,500 feet into the Great Salt Lake. Or maybe not size—scale. *Size determines an object*, Smithson wrote, *but scale determines art*. The scale of *Spiral Jetty* fluctuates, depending on where you are.

Dan was, anyway, a better Alaskan. Camping, for his family, meant hiking in somewhere to pitch a tent; my family drove to campsites. When my new peers asked what Alaska was like, I couldn't say, having not yet figured out the norm to which I should compare it. Discussion of the varying hours of daylight, the duration of seasons, only got me so far. There was a Walmart. There were movie theaters. *I don't know. It's like anywhere.* "Alaska Dan," meanwhile, was possessed of an exotic knowledge—bears, avalanche safety—which, when I was with him in the company of others, was, gratifyingly, shared. In a winter storm, we walked around pushing cars out of snowbanks.

I'd seen, at Dia: Beacon (Dan eventually had a car), smaller Smithson works, ones you couldn't touch. *Map of Broken Glass (Atlantis)* — a pile of broken glass. *Leaning Mirror* — actually two mirrors, back to back, angled into a pile of sand. *Closed Mirror Square (Cayuga Salt Mine Project)* — once, gazing into the trick of the mirror, I got too close, heard the crunch of rock salt underfoot, got warned away.

In Smithson's formulation of "site" and "nonsite," the site was the actual salt mine under Cayuga Lake, outside Ithaca; his *Closed Mirror Square* was one of several nonsites, incorporating the mined salt. *The interior of the museum*, he wrote, *somehow mirrors the site.*

Dan was a physics major turned art major. I took several art classes, but was an English major—more practical. In his studio, Dan made large paintings of Bible stories with robot figures in all the roles. Robots in Eden, robot fathers prepared to sacrifice robot sons. I was making giant urns out of corrugated cardboard I painstakingly distressed. I had nowhere to store them.

For his "mirror displacements," Smithson positioned mirrors in the landscape. These pieces he documented, then dismantled. Mirrors in the dirt can create a tunnel of sky. Gravel heaped against a mirror creates a heap of double size. I don't think mirrors affect scale. Most of Smithson's work was designed to change or disappear entirely over time. (At Dia, they sweep up and maintain the edges of those piles of salt and sand.) *Spiral Jetty* was, for several years, submerged under the Great Salt Lake. Then it reappeared.

In high school, I had dated one of Dan's best friends, and then I briefly dated Dan, and then he dated my best friend, and then we drove across the country. After that, I lose track. But there were times when we slept together and times when he let me stay at his apartment while he slept with someone else, times when we swam in the ocean or rode his two bikes down the concrete steps of a municipal plaza. I moved to Brooklyn. Dan moved back west.

With his wife, Nancy Holt, Smithson made a film called *Swamp* in 1971, shot in a swamp in New Jersey, dense with yellow reeds. Holt advances through the swamp. Smithson tells her where to go.

NEW YORK

There are people now who go out in the desert
and dig a trench and say,
"Look, we've found the earth."
Isamu Noguchi, 1973

THE CAR (SEATTLE)

Soon the second car
came into our lives. We flew to Seattle
to pick it up, a gift from my aunt and uncle.
My cousin had been driving it the past four years
but had recently acquired, second-hand, a Tesla.
He took us for a drive around the block.
I'd seen Teslas on the road, even in our rural town
(we'd moved again)
but never their interiors, and was surprised
by the giant touch-screen on which, after we parked,
we watched the car's computer
playing chess against itself.

Then we drove across the country.
I can tell you, geese are everywhere.

In South Dakota, on the Needles Highway,
we paid our twenty dollars in an envelope
and drove the one-lane tunnel
through a tall, granite spire just as it got dark,
then turned around.

In 1980, the US Supreme Court decided
the government had been wrong in taking back,
through military force, the Black Hills,
promised to the Sioux in perpetuity.
They upheld the decision to grant the tribe
a hundred million dollars,
never claimed.

CHICAGO

I don't know much about ceramics, I said,
slightly coy, to the first ceramicist.
Everybody has a toilet, she said.
We were sharing a bathroom in Nebraska.

The second ceramicist was from South Dakota.
He'd grown up right behind the Corn Palace —
famous for murals made from corn.
And now he was at this birthday party.
Actually, he was a sculptor, dabbling in clay.
I asked if the Corn Palace had influenced his work,
he said no and described his current project, involving
several ceramic cabbages.

The sculptor was anxious,
the kiln had been left unattended.

My Iowa grandma collected
American ceramics, gave the lot to the university.
She liked, she told *Ceramics Monthly,*
the medium's "direct, tactile intimacy" —
the clay passed from hand to hand.

I remember a few pieces
from the house in Des Moines —
in the guest bedroom, the life-size head of a bearded man
being smashed in by a brick.

Self-portrait. The artist taught at UC Davis,
part of the burgeoning scene out there.
Among his other works
are ten clay sculptures of toilets. (An eleventh was destroyed.)
The *Times* reviewed a group show in 1981:
We are left, in short, with some dark thoughts
about the fate of high art
in the California sun.

NEBRASKA

There were two movies that summer
about boys and their horses.
In the first, we didn't cry when the horse was killed,
but near the end. We didn't watch the second one.
I cried all through the trailer, not knowing who might die.
This before Nebraska, where,
driving to the Hy-Vee, we saw two horses standing side by side
but back to front, so that I thought I'd seen
a single being with two heads. Like feelings —
I could never say which were distinct. I only knew
the names of three and sometimes, like my mom —
top of the stairs, late afternoon — I'd holler the wrong one down.

Arizona was the first dance made by Robert Morris, 1963 at Judson Memorial Church. The dance was twenty minutes long, in four sections, accompanied in part by a recording of the artist reading his text "A Method for Sorting Cows." *Two men are required to sort cows in the method presented here.* It was a solo performance.

For the second section, Morris stood at center stage beside a T-like form, which he repeatedly adjusted and retreated from. A lampstand, two sticks. Morris had developed an interest in dance having married the dancer Simone Forti.

(He later left the field at the behest of dancer Yvonne Rainer.)

In 1961 or 2 (sources vary), he'd staged a performance, part of an evening organized by La Monte Young at the Living Theatre. A sculpture he'd built—a plywood rectangular column, *Column* — "performed" a choreography. For three and a half minutes, it stood upright, then it toppled and lay on stage for another three and a half. Morris, in the wings, knocked the column over by pulling an invisible string. Initially, the idea had been for him to stand inside the column and effectuate the fall, but rehearsing the maneuver in Yoko Ono's loft, he'd gashed his eyebrow and ended up in the ER.

Forti had put on a program in that same loft in '61, involving movement, objects, and rules. For one piece, in which Morris participated with artist Robert Huot, she'd installed two heavy screw eyes in the wall. Morris was instructed to lie on the floor and stay there at all costs; Huot, given an 8-foot rope, was instructed to tie him to the wall.

In New York, I'd had an affair with a man who volunteered at the *Dream House*, the sound and light environment created by La Monte Young and Marian Zazeela, his wife. Basically, Young designed the droning sound and Zazeela the magenta light. It was installed in a loft downtown. The man I knew was in charge of asking visitors to remove their shoes, and watched over their stuff while they were inside. When I went to see him there, I realized how much his own apartment—which he kept dim, with colored bulbs, and where he played obscure records—was inspired by this place. I did feel, in his apartment, like I was in an altered state. A couple times, I cat-sat for him, and the place was mine. He never saw where I lived.

Because we mostly met for sex, and because his apartment was small, and mostly bed, it felt, sometimes, like a stage for sex. Also, the sex was more prop-based than I was accustomed to—ropes and gags. I stayed naked, and he drew me baths and adored my flesh and I barely talked and felt like a cat, or a 5-foot tower of fruit.

The critic Michael Fried, in his essay "Art and Objecthood" in *Artforum*, dismissed the "literalist" sculptures of Robert Morris and Donald Judd as "fundamentally theatrical." He quotes from Morris's own *Artforum* essay, "Notes on Sculpture":

One's awareness of oneself existing in the same space as the work is stronger than in previous work, with its many internal relationships. One is more aware than before that he himself is establishing relationships as he apprehends the object from various positions and under varying conditions of light and spatial context.

Fried takes this and argues that literalist art, like theater, exists for an audience. You might say the art is activated by the beholder, who encounters—within this staged environment, under these lights, etc.—a *situation*. But what Morris describes isn't viewer as audience. Both viewer and object are dancers.

After he moved to Seattle,
I couldn't get any other man
to do it right.
No, not like you're mad at me.

TIVOLI

Several members of a wedding
were staying at the inn
where we stopped to see
my most significant ex and his wife.
The four of us went canoeing. He and his wife, together,
carried their boat with such ease,
and Chris and I struggled so much with ours,
that I was comforted to hear — when I stopped to rest
and when my ex came back and took up my position —
that the second boat was, in fact, heavier.

The river was choked with water chestnut.

Later, there was a snake in the yard.
Two men who were otherwise painting the fence
chased it with a rake and a garbage bag and a potato hook
before a man in a tux hopped from a waiting van,
stepped on the snake behind its head,
picked it up and tossed it down the hill.

It was their anniversary, my ex
and his wife's. I hadn't known, that's why they were in town.

DUSSELDORF

Morris was invited to mount a show in Dusseldorf in 1964. Rainer went along. Soon after their arrival, their hosts — gallerist and wife — brought them to a nightclub, where the band played '40s swing. Rainer was half-Jewish and had no interest in this time-travel. Still, they danced.

Morris was gloomy in his studio, re-making plywood and sculpt-metal pieces he'd shown the previous year. In Rainer's sixth-floor walk-up, she was trying to find a new way to move. *No rhythm, no emphasis, no tension, no relaxation.* She started small. It might be just a movement of the eyes.

GERMANTOWN

I didn't know how to read the signs,
the hawk on the ground below the tree,
standing upright, the size of a dog,
the hawk on the fencepost out back
with a snake flashing green in its beak.
Sixteen vultures in the trees
around the scummy roadside pond, four on the roof
of a barn, sunning their outstretched wings.
The goldfinch on the backyard snag.
The wren in our woodstove who scrabbled
against the sooty glass, then went calm
so that I could reach in and grab him —
scooping him up in a dish towel
along with the ashes under him —
and carry him outside,
where he shot from my hands in flight.
The finch in our woodstove three weeks later
who wouldn't settle, who, when I opened the door,
flapped frantic along the ceiling, then perched above the coat rack
on our basket of winter things.
The sparrow who, let out, hopped down
and pecked along the floorboards,
hopped across the welcome mat and out
onto the lawn. Then two wrens at once.
One disappeared like a dove.
When I saw the owl, it was because
the twilight had surprised me.
It started to rain,
I called Chris to come pick me up.
Any time he gets in the car it could kill him.

At the table outside the sanctuary
before Kol Nidre, they looked
for our names on the list.
No Chris.
Or, I suggested, *Christian?*
Ah, they waved us in.

It made no sense
a whole person
could just cease to be.
The only answer was that they didn't.

Returning from Dusseldorf in '64, Rainer had already formed in her head much of *Part of Some Sextets* — a dance for ten people and twelve mattresses, piled about the height of a man. She started conducting rehearsals in December; she and Morris were both among the company.

For the soundtrack, she'd recorded selections from the diary of William Bentley, pastor of a church in Salem, Massachusetts. Volume One begins in 1784. Bentley documents meals he's had, deaths in the town. In 1797, he sees an elephant exhibited. (She drinks a bottle of beer, takes bread from the spectators' pockets.) In 1806, he watches a solar eclipse.

The dancers memorized the words that cued the changes in their movements every thirty seconds:

water now is of a — Bent-over walk
it was taught — One vertical mattress moving back and
    forth
waxwork of same — Quartet
two owls who gave us — "Swedish werewolf"
Newbury and the notes —

Of Morris leaving the performance field, Rainer later wrote: *Now that so much time has elapsed since we were together, it is easy for me to say, "In a way it was too bad."*

Human flies on mattress pile; Formation no. 1 (fling); Formation no. 2 (with "bug squash"); Move pile to other side; Crawl thru below top mattress; Standing figure on top of pile; House lights; Bob's diagonal; Sitting figure; Sleeping figure

Her next work, *Trio A* — a solo performed by three people "simultaneously but not in unison" — had no soundtrack at all, except, at its premiere at Judson Church, the clattering of wooden slats, thrown with regularity from the balcony onto the stage below.

(Don't move like a bird — like an airplane. Not like a faun — like a barrel.)

Rainer and Morris had first performed together in Simone Forti's *See Saw* in December 1960, a performance which ended with Rainer screaming while Morris read a magazine.

In '71, receiving news that he had married someone else, Rainer swallowed pills and landed in the hospital. The sub for her class at SVA brought the students by. Three stories down, on the sidewalk outside, they performed *Trio A* where she could see them.

FRANKFURT

The facial recognition technology
they're using to board the plane
is, of course, strictly optional.

The young family
in whose apartment
I'm staying on my employer's dime
has moved here from Rome. The woman shows me
how to make stovetop espresso
and serves me,
that first morning, two slices
of a chocolate ring-cake, so dry
it turns to powder in my mouth. There will be cake
every morning of my stay here —
the same cake getting drier by the day —
served on a folded paper napkin on a plate.

The second morning, she suggests
that I may take it to my room, so I take the napkin
and, every day, wrap the cake to smuggle out
and deposit it
in a public trashcan. Every day, as I walk,
I end up eating most of it.

Your name, it sounds so German, the ticket woman says.
German Jewish, yes, I say.
Huh. I've never heard it, shakes her head.

Outside a shop, one man holds a window squeegee, double-sided
with the squeegee and the scrubber. He's washing the window
while another man looks on, either learning how to do it
or making sure the first one does it right.
The goal is to not see the glass. I think he's doing great.

I look through
to the phones for sale, tethered to the tables.
I'm waiting to text Chris.
It could be that they're taking turns,
keeping each other company.

A bus pulls up and carries
my reflection away.

The streets are empty, and I'm not sure
when it happened, when it came to seem
actively dangerous to be apart. Alone, I feel
alone, but violently. Like half.

The streets are empty, so I wait with pleasure
in the safety of a line outside a restaurant—
Vietnamese street food, which suggests
wholly different streets.
Once inside, I'm seated
at a table for four
and, after I order, am joined by a man
who, when he orders,
is British. We don't speak. He presumably remains
unaware that we could.

Over the Atlantic, in the row ahead,
a woman attempts to return her breakfast muffin,
unopened in its plastic,
to the flight attendant.
No, it can't be saved.
Everything will be incinerated.

ITHACA

There's the story of the "Earth Art" exhibition at Cornell, 1969. Walter De Maria flew in, through a blizzard, for the opening. A room had been set aside with cartons of dirt, according to his specifications. And when he arrived, he had the dirt dumped out in the center of the floor. He spread it around with a push broom and then, with the handle, wrote in the dirt, GOOD FUCK.

They closed off the room immediately, swept up the soil the next day. It was a school, after all. But the consequence was that Michael Heizer, in protest, withdrew his work, a hole he'd dug in the ground with the dirt piled off to the side. The trouble there was that David Medalla had claimed, for his contribution, the pile of displaced dirt.

Chris was the best man
and wore the seafoam tie
that matched the bridesmaids' dresses.
After his speech,
several guests approached
to suggest he might make money
writing speeches for others.

The day before, on Sunset,
we'd walked into a taco place
and seen another couple from our flight.
We'd noticed them at JFK: around our age
and white and wearing shoes
we also owned. She said, *I'm Rachel.*
And her boyfriend's name
was Matt or something.

My theory of art
is that there should be pleasure
in just hearing the concept,
but added pleasure
in seeing the thing itself.

The Sea World billboard said
Real Feels Amazing.

In a 1961 review, Donald Judd describes
the Robert Motherwell painting *California:*
A wide area left of the center is yellow ocher
tending to Naples yellow. The remainder of the left side
is a chalky cobalt blue of nearly equal value. The intensity of the blue
and the arched span of the yellow ocher compete.
The right is mostly bare canvas bordered by orange.

We were planning our own wedding in Alaska.
This one was in a canyon
in a private zoological garden
and we only saw the ocean from the sky.

In 1970, De Maria developed a proposal for a piece in Hanover, Germany, an entry in an open competition. The idea was to bring in one hundred elephants and give over large areas of the city to them: several miles of streets, special paths through the park. *So that they would become like citizens of the town.*

Because I realized that the city of Hanover and other cities were composed of nothing but buildings, people, and cars ... food and chairs ...

And how did you discover elephants?

The turtle was beside the pond,
ground muddied around her. Slowly, she lowered
one hind leg, then the other,
hollowing a hole
in which to lay her eggs below her.

Down the road, they'd built
the foundation for a home.
It lay now, in the rain,
a kind of wading pool, in waiting.

GERMANTOWN

It was the year of Mona, Lorenzo, and Hattie.
Elena, William, and Ruth. A friend was on bed rest.
A friend miscarried. I asked Mona's mother
what to send Hattie. I walked to the post office,
up through the cemetery. It was the year
we'd planned to marry, the year the fabric of the world
seemed ripped apart and so I hoped my dead mom might return.
I never stopped. My list of names just grew.

Noguchi, as a young man, took a job as tutor to Lincoln Borglum, son of sculptor Gutzon Borglum and namesake of the president whose likeness was his father's specialty. Father and son would eventually work together, carving a 60-foot version of Abraham Lincoln's face into the face of the mountain known to the Lakota as Six Grandfathers.

Noguchi would claim he learned nothing from Borglum of sculpture, though he posed for a Borglum statue of William Tecumseh Sherman, commanding general in the Indian Wars. He carved his own head of Lincoln and lost it.

Although today they aren't as central to his legacy, Noguchi sculpted many heads. In the early years, they made up the greater part of his practice. That practice, over his lifetime, was diverse, encompassing many large public commissions, industrial design (a coffee table that's still, or again, in production—one sits in my sister's Rochester living room), and set designs for Martha Graham, the first of them in 1935 for her *Frontier*—a length of fence and two stretched ropes. He also made two heads of Martha Graham. Berenice Abbott. Gladys Bentley. And one of Ginger Rogers—pink Georgia marble—completed in 1942. The sculptor was in Arizona at the time, interned at Poston War Relocation Center.

Noguchi had, in the days following Pearl Harbor, traveled to Washington, DC. There he met John Collier, commissioner of the Bureau of Indian Affairs. Perhaps, Collier suggested, Noguchi might bring creative vision to an internment camp which was under his direction, located as it was on the Colorado River Indian Reservation. Noguchi picked up his car in California and drove to the desert to help.

But when the internees arrived, he became, at once, one of them. *Naturally. So I was stuck there and couldn't get out for seven months.*

Still, he made plans for a park, a recreation area. *To make the place a park-like place.* Also a cemetery, with chapel, crematory, columbarium.

The trouble was that what Collier wanted and what the War Relocation Authority would countenance were two different things. Collier wanted to make it into— What the Mojave Indians couldn't do, he thought the Japanese could do: make the place blossom.

Noguchi developed an interest in Native American earthen mounds, evident in his 1947 design for the unrealized *Sculpture to be Seen from Mars* — giant mounds in the form of a face, to be built in the desert somewhere, the nose a mile long. Future-minded, he'd initially titled it *Memorial to Man*.

We only have photos of the model in sand. You can see them in Long Island City at the Noguchi Museum, founded by the artist himself. I walked there with my friend, over the bridge, on a day when we were feeling very sad, and when, if I'm remembering correctly, admission was free. And we sat in the garden, sun on the stones and on our clothes. *There is a time passage to stone not unlike our own.*

The horse was in its yard,
on its side, lying down.
Legs bent and hooves off the ground.
Its mouth—

Two more horses stood by.
This was outside Rochester.

It was wrong
to measure loss by size.
Wrong to measure loss
by human grief,
to see the house cat
on the highway
as different from a possum
or the birds
fallen far from the road.

I'd offered criticism when he came to me for help. The sky was gray and the drops, halfway between snow and rain, fell lightly. I ran around the reservoir. At its center was a fountain, recirculating water which erupted up, cascaded white. Chris was struggling in my sister's house. He'd been loved so poorly in his past that the standard for me now felt both too high and deplorably low. I faltered when the man approaching stopped and turned to follow me the other way around.

On our visit in the summer, we'd run this route together and seen families with folding chairs and coolers full of beverages, here on Cobbs Hill to watch the sunset. Now it was December, but the grass was green and on Highland Ave the decorations seemed divorced from the season and only an expression of politics or personality.

The nieces loved him so much he worried he would hurt them. He had a mind like that. Mara had the idea she couldn't enjoy her marble track without him. He was usefully tall and held their hands as they walked along fallen trees, balancing, in Washington Grove, just down from the reservoir. He hadn't known I had to stand on tiptoe to hold him when he panicked, to put my arms around his neck and run my hands down his back.

The reservoir, supposedly, could fill every bathtub in the city twice daily for two months. My sister's children bathed somewhat irregularly; I admired this. Once there were black bears here. The Seneca set ground-fires to enhance the understory, attracting wild turkeys and elk. White settlement ended the practice. Maples, cherries, and tulip trees grew, filling in the canopy, closing out the light. Hickories vanished. Chestnuts succumbed to chestnut blight. Then came Dutch elm disease and butternut canker. Schoolchildren planted sugar maples to replace the chestnuts. Invasive Norway maple shut out reproduction of native trees. Brown-headed cowbirds parasitized others' nests—

Or if we were in bed—or atop twin mattresses, pushed together on the floor of my sister's study—he could rest his high head, novelly, on my chest, and I would stroke his hair and tell him it was okay, it was just his brain, it didn't happen.

THE MOON

Bausch had her dancers create movements
to express ideas, experiences.
*"The moon?" I depicted the word with my body
so she could see and feel it.*

For *Vollmond*, a giant chunk
of rock evokes a lunar landscape.
Water fills a wide, shallow trough in the stage,
reflecting the dancers' movements.
Rain falls intermittently.

Dancers climb the rock. Dancers climb
other dancers. Rain falls and men with poles
sort of row themselves across the stage,
skate-sliding on the surface.
Now they swim-slide on their bellies
in the overflowing trough.

I watched this, finally, in *Pina*, the movie,
while Chris listened to something
in the other room.

Dancers wade into the trough,
scoop water up in buckets
and splash it on the giant rock,
like trying to save a whale.
They throw water on each other,
on themselves, their clothes are drenched.

The water stuff is primal. There are other
heterosexual antics, too, not in the film.
A man races against the clock to undo
a woman's bra. Men pour liquid
from bottles from great heights,
overfilling women's glasses.

Vollmond was one of Pina's last works.
Of the performances after her death, critics expressed
a certain weariness, alongside great esteem.
Nothing remains new.

She requested a gesture related to "joy"—
joy or the pleasure of moving.
From the movement I presented,
she created an entire scene.

Rolf Borzik first flooded the Wuppertal stage for a work called *Arien* in 1979, eight months before he died at thirty-six. Leukemia. He and Pina lived together for a decade, worked together to create the Tanztheater's look, or looks: women with loose hair, braless in filmy dresses; sometimes partial nudity; something close to street clothes; slightly shabby eveningwear.

Borzik's sets included earth and water, a carpet of dead leaves, a full dead tree, a bathtub, plush furniture on casters, and, when Pina asked, a hippopotamus—a puppet, or a rubbery two-man costume, but persuasive. Also realistic crocodiles.

The double bill of *Café Müller* and *The Rite of Spring* shows two different modes—the dirt of *Rite of Spring*, the spare but realist restaurant with tall glass doors on both sides and in back, with a revolving door beyond. There are tables and too many chairs. (Pina's parents ran a restaurant attached to a hotel in Solingen.)

Pina herself danced in *Café Müller*—though she spends much of her time against a wall, a ghostly presence. Her eyes are closed and when she moves, her arms are angled out in front of her, palms up.

Rolf also performed—the only time I know of. As a second woman moves across the stage, he throws the chairs aside to clear her path.

When *Arien* came to Brooklyn in 1985, four thousand gallons of water trucked in from New Jersey and meant to be reused each night turned out to be contaminated. New water was found.

CAYUGA LAKE

There's no snow in Ithaca
but I get the idea this is unusual
from the shovels and cross-country skis
people keep by their front doors.

The Cayuga Lake salt mine is still in operation,
closed today. We lightly trespass
on the property.
Chris says to remind him
what Smithson did out here.

Mostly the salt goes to de-icing roads—
half for roads in New York State. They mine
two million tons per year and estimate
they have a few more decades.
Some women are gathered in a shale pit
by the car. They show us how to look.

Back on campus, the lake where Dennis Oppenheim
cut a path through ice with a chainsaw in '69
is mostly open water, the ice nowhere thicker
than a windshield.

I hold a rock that holds the mold
of several tiny scallops
and the ridges of a trilobite.

There's ice on the moon. There may be subsurface
saltwater lakes on Mars.
Most extrasolar planets
are older than ours, and so if we imagine
that civilizations everywhere emerge
on similar timescales, any one to contact us
will have found a way
to survive
much longer than we may.

Sculpture is most pleasing at a human scale.
Judd was dismissive
of Morris's early objects, but: *The horizontal slab*
suspended at eye level does work.
It is a good idea.

It's the same reason people appreciate deer.
In Alaska, we only had moose, giant,
impossible to know
what they're thinking.

White-tailed deer in New York State
had disappeared almost completely
by the mid-1800s,
their habitat destroyed.
Tourists in the Catskills went to deer parks just to see them.
Chris learned this in a comprehensive history of the region
he read most nights while I slept.

(I hurt him once by denigrating
the mountains themselves,
belligerently homesick.)

Often, on walks through the cemetery, I'd surprise
a family of deer—they'd run, jumping over headstones
to the trees.

Judd in '64: *Morris's pieces exist after all, as meager as they are.*
Things that exist exist, and everything is on their side. They're here,
which is pretty puzzling.

A museum, a deer park,
a family,
a dance troupe,
a cemetery. Company.

MARS

I ran into her a few years after moving to New York, in the stairwell of PS1. She was a performance artist now, she told me, which made some sense. We knew each other from doing youth theater, in our youth. Later I found a video online. In it—as I remember it—she held a pane of glass, dropped it to the floor where it shattered, then undressed, writhed among the shards, and smeared the walls with blood from her cut-up breasts. I resolved to follow her career, and created a Google alert, but after that, there were never any relevant hits, which I would later realize was because she had begun performing under an assumed name.

We had done youth theater in Alaska, and I was disappointed to find no mention of Alaska in her professional bio. I hadn't known she'd been born in California, and this was the art-world standard, to give only the year and location of your birth. But surely Alaska had informed her practice, her later interest in colonization and climate catastrophe.

She was a few years older than I was and, as a teenager, had been generous with me. She once beat me out for the role of Anne Frank. The role was double-cast: one girl was Anne-the-girl, the other was the diary. (It was more successful than it sounds.) We auditioned in pairs, roughly matched in appearance, so that my audition partner—also older than me, but diminutive— was the girl whom I was otherwise most often up against for roles, and who most often prevailed, possessed of undeniable charisma. If we had, in this case, prevailed together, she would no doubt have been girl-Anne, and I the diary. My early success in the theater was based mostly on excellence within my age group at cold reading. But I was, at the time, closest to Anne's real age and felt spiritually close to her, beyond just being Jewish. The performance artist and her tall partner won out. My double and I ended up as Anne's schoolmates, disappearing from the play once the Frank family entered the secret annex, and returning as extras in the camp. The artist carried the show. It was, for her, in fact, a return. In an earlier production—the company tended to repeat its successes—she had played the role of Anne's sister, Margot. My older sister played Anne Frank.

My double would die young, in a motorcycle accident. I attended the memorial, held in the same auditorium where we had all performed together, on the campus of the local university.

The university had loaned the space, but had its own fairly robust theater arts program, and I was thinking about it on a late-summer visit to my dad, walking through the campus near his house. The air smelled like smoke from fires to the north and south. The sitting governor had recently proposed outrageous cuts to the university—aimed, people said, at defunding climate science, but usually the arts go first. The cuts would also necessitate the closure of rural community campuses, which allowed students to pursue education while living with their families, in their villages, and offered courses in nursing, social work, construction management, snow machine repair, plant identification, traditional basket weaving, net mending, whale biology, and understanding the Alaska Native Claims Settlement Act.

The performance artist, when I found her again online, had become quite successful, with a solo exhibition at a major museum, grounded in inquiry into the potential colonization of Mars, so often hopefully discussed as an option for the continuation of the species after the depletion of resources on Earth and the mining of the asteroid belt. The exhibition's centerpiece was a durational performance, ten days long, during which the artist and two others lived and slept in the museum, in a 3-foot-wide space between two panes of window-glass—a simulation of life in a closed ecological system, like a spacecraft, or a biodome on Mars. The three women had ten days' supply of food, a treadmill and a composting toilet. They collected their urine and recycled greywater. They grew edible sprouts. They banged the dishes and danced under red light.

The artist called this "real theater." If you live on a set, it's not really a set. I had left theater after high school and possessed now no real theory of performance, which I would broadly define as stuff you do with your body. But I'd say that "theater" is distinguished by imagination—when acting, the actions of your body are dependent on imagined external realities. In our youth, for her performance as Anne Frank in the "secret annex," the artist imagined life and first love in a confined space while Jews were being rounded up outside. In the "biodome," she cooked ramen. She watered the plants. She arranged crystals on a shelf. She took sponge baths. She adjusted the surveillance cameras. She cleaned and swept the floors. She colored her shoes red. She had a few items she'd brought—a special copper spoon. She looked out the windows. She stretched.

At the end of the ten days, the women carried out their waste. The scheduled culminating event was a panel discussion, moderated by the exhibition's curator, and the women answered questions from the audience about collective living and isolation. But the artist's behavior was growing increasingly erratic. She spasmed and stumbled. For a while, she quietly humped the wall, and then she was beating herself against it. There was grunting and screaming, sounds of climax and labor—all three women participants now in a violent sexual frenzy. Then they left the room.

GERMANTOWN

I packed the books first,
topping off the boxes
with sweatshirts, kitchen towels.

Then most of the dishes. Dried beans
and spices. I tried to finish
perishables.

Chris was on the road and I got pictures
of the road, the lakes.

Solo beginning with shifting weight

Duet: Bob's entrance
Rope duet (with rope)
Vague movements
Racing walk

Rope movements 1 thru 4

Duet: Corridor solo
Duet: Diagonal run to end

I woke up sideways in the bed.

THE CATSKILLS

How far to the falls? Chris asked
the young family coming toward us
on the trail.
*You're very very very very
very very close.*

ACKNOWLEDGEMENTS

I'm grateful to my poetry teachers, and want to especially thank Kate Angus, Catherine Barnett, Terrance Hayes, Ed Hirsch, Maureen McLane, and Geoffrey Nutter. And Meghan O'Rourke, for so much. I'm grateful, also, to Bill Deresiewicz, who encouraged my writing before I found poetry. I'm grateful to my classmates at NYU, especially to Aria Aber, Ama Codjoe, Isabelle Conner, Alexandria Hall, Francisco Márquez, Momina Mela, Jessie Modi, Madeleine Mori, Karisma Price, and Leigh Sugar, for their generous engagement with my work and for the beauty of their poems. And to Maggie Millner and Eleanor Wright, steadfast and brilliant companions and guides. I'm grateful to my Bread Loaf cohort, particularly poets Taneum Bambrick, Michaela Cowgill, and Dylan Weir. For fellowship in writing and much else, I'm grateful to Jake Fournier, Callie Garnett, Jess Laser, Dan Poppick, Aaron Thier, Sarah Trudgeon, Jeff Whitney, and Hannah Withers. And I'm grateful to Eric Amling and Sarah Jean Grimm; I wouldn't have finished this book if not for them. For friendship in the tender early days in New York, and now, I'm forever grateful to Kelly Burdick, Teddy Goff, Jon Hood, Priyanka Jacob, Ajay Kishore, Marcel Przymusinski, Michael Rae Grant, and Mark Schulte. For deep friendship across distance, I'm grateful to Anastatia Curley and Maggie Doherty. I'm indebted to Ming-qi Chu for so much that's good in my life, and in particular for reminding me, in a difficult time, that poetry was something that had often made me feel better. I'm grateful to the wonderful Vince Dorie. I'm grateful to the women of Alaska, lifelong friends

Priya Keane, Krysta Kurka, Diana Patton, Kait Reiley, and Erin Weidner. And to Francesca Du Brock, for making art alongside me, and for reconnecting me to the North when I needed it most. I'm grateful to my former colleagues at Bloomsbury, especially Anton Mueller and Kathy Belden, and my current colleagues at JMH Scouting and *The Yale Review*, all of whom have taught me to be a better reader. I'm grateful to everyone at the Studios at MASS MoCA, the Vermont Studio Center, and Castello di San Basilio, where parts of this book were written. I'm grateful to the people— and the animals and plants—of Germantown, New York, where the bulk of this book was written. And to dear friends throughout the Hudson Valley, and all the other friends and loved ones in these pages. I'm grateful to the following editors, who have published excerpts of this work, some of them in different forms, or have otherwise encouraged me in the right direction: Aria Aber at *Astra Quarterly*, Catherine Blauvelt at the NYPL, Jennifer Chang at *New England Review*, Will Frazier, Hannah Hirsh, and Natasha Rao at *American Chordata*, Alexandria Hall at *Tele-*, Keetje Kuipers at *Poetry Northwest*, Thomas Mira y Lopez at *Territory*, Ange Mlinko at *Subtropics*, Donald Revell at *Colorado Review*, David Ulin at *Air/Light*, and Michael Wiegers at *Narrative*. I'm extraordinarily grateful to Terrance Hayes, Robyn Schiff, and Jenny Xie for reading this book and offering their support. I'm unendingly, inexpressibly grateful to Louise Glück for all her kindness, for her trusted advice, and for helping me to trust myself, and to Bennet Bergman, for his passion and care; I couldn't have asked for a better publisher. I'm grateful to my grandmother, Joan Mannheimer, for helping to instill my interest in art. To all my extended family. To Sharon, Scott, Josh, and my beloved nieces. I'm profoundly grateful to my father, David, and my sisters, Katie and Sara; I cherish them beyond words. To my mother, Carol, who was kind and brave, and to whom this book is dedicated. And to Chris Schlegel, a wonder, for making this life with me.

ABOUT THE AUTHOR

Rachel Mannheimer was born and raised in Anchorage, Alaska, and lives in New Haven, Connecticut, where she works as a literary scout and as a senior editor for *The Yale Review*. This is her first book.